5-29-24

Moon Jar

Moon Jar

poems

DIDI JACKSON

Red Hen Press | *Pasadena, CA*

Book design by Mark E. Cull

Library of Congress Cataloging-in-Publication Data

Names: Jackson, Didi, 1970– author.
Title: Moon jar : poems / Didi Jackson.
Description: First edition. | Pasadena, CA : Red Hen Press, [2020]
Identifiers: LCCN 2019041297 | ISBN 9781597098175 (trade paperback) | ISBN
9781597098182 (ebook)
Subjects: LCSH: Bereavement—Poetry. | LCGFT: Poetry.
Classification: LCC PS3610.A3486 M66 2020 | DDC 811/.6—dc23
LC record available at https://lccn.loc.gov/2019041297

The National Endowment for the Arts, the Los Angeles County Arts Commission, the
Ahmanson Foundation, the Dwight Stuart Youth Fund, the Max Factor Family Foun-
dation, the Pasadena Tournament of Roses Foundation, the Pasadena Arts & Culture
Commission and the City of Pasadena Cultural Affairs Division, the City of Los An-
geles Department of Cultural Affairs, the Audrey & Sydney Irmas Charitable Founda-
tion, the Kinder Morgan Foundation, the Meta & George Rosenberg Foundation, the
Allergan Foundation, the Riordan Foundation, Amazon Literary Partnership, and the
Mara W. Breech Foundation partially support Red Hen Press.

First Edition
Published by Red Hen Press
www.redhen.org

for Major

Contents

I
Your Husband Was a City in a Country of Sorrow

II
Another city will be found, better than this.

Rakomelo

III

Eternal City

Moon Jar

Signs for the Living

Sometimes, after the last snow in May,
after the red-winged blackbird clutches the spine
of the cattail, after he leans forward, droops
his wings and flashes his epaulets, I imagine
shouldering the yellow center lines of the road.

Near the recently thawed pond, within a long
channel of construction, a man holding a sign.
One side says slow, the other stop.
Joy and sorrow always run like parallel lines.

Inside the house, when I leave the lights on,
small white moths come like a collection of worship,
pulsing their wings up and up the window,
as if in a frenzied trancelike dance,
some dervishes, others the penitent on shaky knees.

The first few years after my husband's suicide
I wanted to be the penitent.
I thought I deserved all the pain I could feel.
The drill of road work in late summer
was a welcome grinding music.
Now the yellow center lines are flung like braids behind me.

I
Your Husband Was a City
in a Country of Sorrow

*In my body the memories were lodged. This writing
is a dim bulb on a black cord in the examiner's room.*

ॐ

*I prefer you do not attempt to read it. I cannot help but feel responsible
for your discomfort. So as you read, you will feel me tugging it from
your hands.*

—Toi Derricotte

I'm never finished answering the dead.

—Li-Young Lee

Almost Animal

after Käthe Kollwitz

I heard they no longer sew eyelids of the dead shut.
At the morgue, I busied myself counting
the lacerations on my husband's neck and wrists.
I wore sunglasses and a light jacket
and pressed my palm to his wrapped chest.

After the dried blood was wiped from his face, his jaw was set
with a piece of string. They tried to leave a natural appearance.
I wanted to smooth his clothes; I wanted to clean his hair.
His throat was a village, my palm an iron of matrimony.
I wanted to burn the holding room, jar and sell the ashes.

At home, the hours layered like moths.
I didn't eat and slept some nights. This was my way
of waging war. There was nothing left for me.
I carried him on my back and over my shoulders. I carried him
across my forehead and between my shins.
But it didn't matter; he was going right into the fire.
I should have been the one to have prepared his body.

kill lies all

After his death,
my hair did not grow,
my nails peeled and flaked,
my bones were lifted into a sack
upon my legs. Even my muscles
decayed from the lack
of wild oranges and sweet tea.
This was the new myth of my life.

When visiting Spain, a cricket was loose
in my kitchen, its chirp was
like my name, like the words *yes, yes.*
But what could a dead woman know
of *yes*? That summer, one cricket
became two, two became four.
It was then I memorized
the trill and grind of my name.
Like a vandal with a can of red spray paint,
I could scrawl the words *kill lies all*
across my *Guernica*. Who will
be the bull, the horse? Who
the severed head and arm?
Under the bald lamp, like an eye,
I will expose old scars and breast-feed
a shadow of myself.

Killing Jar

There are days
I go to the mailbox
and find letters
from my dead husband
translating for me his suicide:
the cold blade softened into cursive,
his fear licked onto the stamp,
as the return address: the date of his death.
I look forward to these letters.
Some are addressed to my son,
I collect and keep those.
At times this is a greedy act,
but he is too young.
I see my body asleep in my son's body,
my eyes behind his eyes.
But now I worry that there is distortion
like Parmigianino's *Self Portrait
in a Convex Mirror*, his hand
slightly reaches out to me,
slightly curls back into itself.

When I was a girl, my uncle
mailed to me framed collections
of mounted butterflies.
Blue morpho. Tigerwing.
Malachite. Moon Satyr.
These are all names my husband
could take now. I imagine him
as Goldman's Euselasia
or the Great Eurybia.

I know that to kill a butterfly,
you use a killing jar.

Because they are so fragile,
sometimes butterflies batter
themselves in the killing jar.
At night, this makes me wonder
about the mixing
spoons in the bowl,
the tangles of the dough
such small, temporary fights.

For a clean kill, it is better
to first stun a butterfly
by pinching its thorax.
But you must practice to get
this method right,
so it is recommended to try
it on common moths or butterflies
you are not concerned about.
Pinch smartly between your finger
and thumb like tweezing a piece of sky.

Honing

A sharp knife is a safe knife.
There is a difference between honing a knife
and sharpening it. The metal rod that stands
in the center of my knife block only hones.
I can hone my skills, perfect them over time.
I might hone granite, hone my French,
hone rock climbing and lovemaking.
When I sharpen an edge, I grind away
at the metal blade, the stainless steel
burrs become smooth like a trained voice
or like following the rules.

But after his suicide, I collected all the blades
from the kitchen. I admired the heft
of the chef's knife, the balance of the tang.
It only takes a twenty-degree angle to sharpen
the length of a blade. The day he died
I sliced a loaf of bread, some cheese to sit out
waiting for a return never to come.
Where did I think all the blood came from?
To hone is to re-center the blade.
To sharpen is to animate the wind.

After the Suicide

The baby grand needs to be tuned.
It sits in the corner like a chained bear,
pitch and octave like matted fur full of grit.
Even so, my son goes to the piano daily,
dragging out the music by its papery edge
with practice and patience. Early mornings,
before breakfast, the throat
of our home fills like gardenias in bloom.

When he finally masters Chopin, I am sure
the *Nocturnes* harbor all my son's grief.
They do mine. I wonder in what key the dead
would prefer a song? There are several
tiny scratches on the lid of the piano
and one long gash on the fallboard.
He does not know the manner of death,
the stabbing and slicing—practice cuts,
the coroner called them. The irony
is lost on my son, but not on me.

Directions for My Son on His Birthday

I cup my hands to hold your youth.
I try to show you how to do the same.

It takes decades of practice to get this right,
and by then it is always too late.

Yesterday, a man stabbed a homeless man on Church
Street. At dinner, we tuck this story between

bites of salmon, pieces of song by Fleetwood Mac
melting from the speaker. It rained

all day today; I told you
that I always thought I'd have another baby.

In truth, I knew I was only good
for one. No matter how hard you press

the outer edges of your palms and pinkies together,
they will always leak. You should know

that you can't hold water in your palm for long.
Don't put yourself in a spot where

you'll have to carry all you will need.
At dusk, we count four rabbits on the back lawn

and I consider if it is a sign
only to watch the stalking feral tabby

turn them to humble bronze, heavy
and frozen and hopefully downwind.

At least once a year, you should close
your cupped hands like a book.

Not to worry. Hinged,
they always open again.

Ascension

The blue jays lay claim
to the raspberry bush
arriving in groups of four or five:
one holds a rubied berry in its beak
and feeds it up in the white pine to another
as if placing the bones of the canonized
into a gilded reliquary, and I think of the saint
for the mentally ill, beheaded by her father
who was blinded by desire
for his daughter; what became of him
but the colorless thread of grief,
a blind man who opened his eyes too late.

All grievances come to a head
like a champagne bottle shaken and shaken,
the cork volunteering its own release—my husband alone
in a hotel room, after the pills came the decision to empty himself,
the deep red circling his body becoming his own nimbus:
an ascension of sorts. I worried for his soul
and if he'd dwell in Hell: Boschian beasts
perched and ready for torture, exploding cities,
tooth-and-tonged caves waiting for the damned.

I hear the jays mocking a poor chickadee's attempt
at reaching the fruit; it's no wonder in legend
they are the devil's servant not to be encountered on a Friday
as they might be found fetching sticks
down to Hell, but I know better, I can tell,
they do no one's bidding but their own.

Your Husband Was a City in a Country of Sorrow

Your husband was a city in a country of sorrow.
As some trees stay green all year,
others drop their leaves like clothes,
the sky sheds its light like a shirt,
and stars fall like socks.
A body heavy and jaundiced
slides down a wall, naked,
leans to one side or the other,
stiffens slightly in that pose
until you find him, your eyes slipping
in blood, the towels untouched.
He was a seed in a nest of grief.
He was lead in a river of silence.
He was a finger in the fist of failure.

The Morgue

They say evening will come
with lazy feet and arms
hanging at its side,

a man in a box burned
like his last hymn,
the body emptied days ago.

Pacing the sky,
the stars are caged beasts,
Fauves of the night.

The way into the morgue: a knock
and a slice, the ash's yellow leaves:
like his eyes they explain the silence.

The pleasure of his hair and skin
in a cold room:
the mockingbird's summer

drains into fall:
the night drains
into perpetual night.

The jaundiced fabric
of verbs: action and action
is woven to cover

the sun, sewn tight
like the lips of the dead.
Nothing at all of courage:

just a blanket folded neat
as a napkin at the foot of a corpse.

Slip

The cat slips
out the window, the thread slips
past the eye, the sun slips
into the stratus, the letter *s* slips
past my tongue, the lead slips
beyond the drop of the *y*, a steal pyramid slipped
in & out of a utility knife, the blade slipped
into the skin on his wrist and neck, the *whisper song* of jays slips
from beak to beak, tree to tree, he slipped
down the bathroom wall, I slip
on ice I do not see, the temperature slips
below zero, our photo slips
from its place in the frame, the river slips
past the storm-downed tree, I slipped
past a wedge of light to enter the morgue, I let it slip:
suicide, the blooms of the lilacs slip
into a purple and white parade, at the end of the day I slip
out of my body.

The Almond Bush

He had the many tongues of the wind chime.
For months, he talked to me through its hollow tubes,
the branches of the elm a medium
rolling back its leaves like a hundred eyes.

What did he need as he entered death
and do I owe him anything?

Now, when I walk through the house, I shut
doors, cabinets, any drawer that is open.
No light bulbs can be bare, no cords can show
from under the couch or behind a chair.
In this way I keep my spinal nerve,
even if I hear him call from the garden.
During a storm, I am only skeleton strong.

One night, I perched like a moth in the corner of our room
and waited for him to come back to himself.
Instead, he walked through the red doors of daybreak
and never returned.

What is the difference between surviving and living?
I dream of the wasps that visit our almond bush,
a sticky scent in the dead of summer. In my dream
I catch several, jar their sting and lack of song.
Do all men take lovers? He killed himself for this.
My grief piles like old bedding.

After a Visit to New Smyrna Beach, Florida

Even the ocean's relentless roar
can be a kind of wail, the stars above
the breakers: tiny archipelagos of agony.
I can grieve here or in the North.
At dawn, crows gather at the ocean's edge.
Such a contrast to the day's white
gulls who, papery and weightless, hover
above the whimper and moan of the shoreline.
I don't like to write about the ocean.
It reveals its emotions too easily.
But here I am. Closer to the place
of your death than I prefer to be.
It rains every afternoon
and thunderheads build like ashy skyscrapers.
The ocean litters its shores with its dead
that visitors collect in buckets and pockets
and carry home. I never buried you.
Instead, I gave the urn to your family:
you believed in no god;
I believed in the clockwork of waves,
still do I guess. Hoping they somehow will
hurry time, or at least for now deafen it.

Summer

We call it heat-lightning
when summer nights camera-flash
the silhouettes of the already black thunderheads
and lightning threads the cloth of the sky.
No clap. No roll. Just silence and show.

His body was rigid in death
and cold from storage.
In a week, the blood had pooled
in unexpected places,
the pattern of small incisions
like drops of dried honey.
I remember him in life
as easily as in death,
before he was yellow
and hollow.

This is the problem with the living:
we think the night has its own wings,
comes to us nodding like a storm buoy.
We think the silence
keeps us safe from the lightning:
a candle and a blanket
are all we think we need.
But in the morning
we are the ones left
to sweep away the scorched
wings of moths.

Lot's Wife

I have rummaged in steel cages, cut my finger
while I carved the apple of my health until the peel
lived, dancing like a string from my nipple.
Across my shoulders, my black shawl
measured his length, his width in death.
Quit the landscape of knives.
I have tasted salt too many times,
worn a backpack filled with slag and fortune,
planted teeth and bone in a summer garden,
guzzled everything red and splintered.
I've roped a wrist and neck in my netted
dreams. Cut out paper dolls but shredded their clothes.
Granted my eyes a flood of blood,
switched from screams to whimpers.
What could have steadied his hand? Not my lips or breasts.
Broken branches from the winged elm stack like a trap.
Those who walk with me may not look back.

A Poem in Reverse

The rosemary and thyme return to seed.
The chimes absorb their song,
the metal pipes consume the notes,
drink in the air of years.
The minutes go backwards:
soil and ash become wood.
I feel his palms on mine.
A ring slips from my finger
into his pocket,
his suit suddenly too large.
The box cutter in his hand
at the hotel finds its way back
into a bag he begins to pack.
Gulls fly back across the Atlantic,
storms shrink into small shells
of wind and rain and he
slides back up a wall
in the bathroom.
The mirror returns his reflection
and the fluorescent lights
cast a yellow glow of disbelief.
I unclench a fist, shave
my words closely, snatch at the limes
in the garden as they return to blossoms:
white and patient among glossy leaves,
like the sugar of so many songs,
drunk and immune to time.

Encaustic

Trying to turn each soaked page, welding
his voice inside each line, a cloisonné of language,
planting the glass of his life within the gold
rim of my day, swallowing the gems:

he lived and lived until he didn't:
a gold spun kiss in the white morning,
straw, an early fall, a spell.

I heard the police say
the hotel room carpet was soaked
from the bathroom to the door.
They didn't mean with water.
I will ask to see his death
photos, to know the body I knew in life.

In a matter of a day,
I will be the white of wax
and the color of all pigment.
I will be a corridor
and in me time will whir
like mosquitos in mid-July.

The Parable of the Hole in the Earth

That summer she was sure she saw the earth split open. Birds who fly south for the winter stayed all year. They recognized what was in the hole and so they couldn't leave.

Not yet.

And she couldn't sleep for all the birdsong. Like monks, they chanted at all hours, their voices poured into the mourning like melted bronze into a mold that cracks after only one use. Her doubts came to her as twins, and they spoke the trilled language only the red-wing and the grackle know. She answered in a metallic voice that sounded like chimes. She knew it was an ancient and soon-to-be-forgotten language.

Everyone Says I Should Write a Love Poem

but I am too busy. My dog is too loyal.
A war could break out any minute;
it might be a Civil War.
I don't know how to make charms
and I've never owned an amulet.
These horns and hooves never let me
rest comfortably. It is better
when looking at sculpture and fine art
to keep moving. The moon is a pod
of milkweed, the seeds are the stars.
An emerald beetle is destroying ash trees.
Blood pools in surprising areas away
from the mortal wounds. In death,
his eyes were closed and glued.
He could not see me even when he
was alive. My father wanted to be a preacher.
So did his father. Now, when I make the bed
I have to tap his pillow four times
just like this:
                    I find clementines too bitter.
My son remembers the last words he said
to him. My scars feel like fish moving
under my flesh. The winds are too strong
in my new home. We lose power often.
I have fallen in love
                    with the snow.

Finally, Green Is January

On the sixth day after his death
she enters the home that used to be theirs
and lies on a bed that today was made
for her, by her.
It is the summer she prayed for more color.
On the third day she looks at her hips,
her breasts: two empty vows.
She wakes only with herself.
It is the summer of space and line.
The wind wants too much.
A voice in the language of chimes forbids her to eat,
to hate yellow, to tug fistfuls of her hair.
Her legs pause when cleaning the dead hydrangea
of funeral bouquets from the floor, dried blue bullets.
Branches will grow from her eyes, leaves on her fingertips,
and bark will wrap her torso like a lover.
On the fifth day she says she wants a wife
someone to mend the holes
someone to lie down for her
someone to count the scissors and knives
        at the beginning and end of each day
someone to complain to God and the birds
        who refuse the seed in the mornings.
Finally, green is January and she is alive.
She pauses on naked feet.

The Florida Sandhill Crane

By wings whose shapes
are but half a heart?
      Feathers oiled with
      country clubs and
gasps of delight? Not for these
the sandhill crane
shakes her beaded voice.

Gauche and gangrene,
she is the gatekeeper of gibe,
      a cement-grey song
      edged and pocked in grassy
fields, a frock of scarlet
over her eye, her own letter
to time and her maker;

a bow, a leap, all a dance
to the heavens and the blue
      plastic tarps mapping
      the devil in a state
of wind and rain,
a crucifix in her throat
to scratch the itch of her fable.

Fruit flies darn the citrus fallen
and rotten in the late spring
      she side-steps and heads
      for the wetlands, to a river
that flows North pierced with blossoms

and the song of Marsyas,
a Suprematist's White on White, blossom on flesh,

small Corinthian dreams gargle in her throat,
her voice of leaves and muck
        folded up in an awkward flight,
            a frieze of battles and victories
lining the sky as if in a couplet
of straight lines, as if she could know she would wed
the palette of one into a mural of two.

II
Another city will be found, better than this.
—*C.P. Cavafy*

This is what it means to be mythological.
—T.R. Hummer

Rakomelo

i

Serifos Aubade

At dawn, you might come
to my doorway framed
and thirsty. On your lips
you'll keep a promise
of apricots and the Meltemi winds.
My late husband couldn't forgive
the morning, so he took his own life.
What would you tell him? Would you speak
of the sand in our sheets?
      We never know what comes next.
The sun dusts off the moon but only halfheartedly,
then kneels like a lover over the sea.
By now we watch the silhouette of a bird
absorbing the oarsman slowly,
drawing him away from the shore.

ii

Lia Beach

No gulls arrive.
The waves on the beach are fluted and clocked.
Bathers stop at the edge, take off their clothes.
A woman collects the trash. Nightfall will come
and the shore will close without leaving a message.
I crouch in the perfect hour but cannot decide
what road to take. My neck is burnt
from the day's sun; my shirt is balled
in my fist, and I collect shells like a pilgrim
trying to buy my way home. But there is only
one path and there is no home.

iii

Warning Signs

The fringe on the mala beads frays
after daily doses of short caresses
and empty, cloudless chants.
They were made for use: *utilitarian*.
I use that word in the art history class
I teach when I refer to Minoan clay pots
or Merovingian fibula.
I know my hands are utilitarian too,
but when I bring them together to pray,
they become purely ornamental.

iv

Poem Beginning with a Line after Yehuda Amichai

Past the window in the room where we make love
waves follow one another like lines of laundry
as the cliffs unfold, spilling like bolts of cloth into the bay,
and it is the anise, they say, the snails
are after, defining the roads of Serifos
like small-change coins, curled and climbing fierce
as soldiers up each stalk in numbers so thick
they could be plucked like white berries ripe
with June, and they too would taste of licorice
succulent in a time of honey and nettles.

v

Reading Sappho on Serifos

Please don't ask of the beekeeper,
the boxes stacked, *tholos* of hive and honey,
the priest white suit he wears, masked,
the flat plate of the sky as it cracks
against the coffee-colored cliffs behind him.
Don't ask of the pines gloved in green,
the water coated in a Biblical blue.
And don't ask to claim the words
for the gulls, hovering patient as paper.

No, don't ask of the stone walls veining the hills
ancient and heavy with hesitation,
the terraces carved and coupled,
the roads only suggestions,
the beaches loose translations.

Please don't ask to hear: *light*.
Don't ask to hear: *I cannot imagine the future*
of any girl who looks on the light of the sun.
Don't ask of the sun.

vi

In the Morning

In the morning, the echo of the previous day
lingers like a shadow on the kitchen wall.
Someone will bring in the dead, will clean
and mend wounds that will never heal, will set
a table with cloth and silver for all to eat *in memoriam*.
The silver will not be polished, and the dog
will stare in the direction of the sea where
all the answers sink like lures, shiny and brilliant,
uselessly swaying like slowly nodding heads.

vii

The Monastery of Taxiarches

> *you turn in your bed*
> *to watch the moon rise, and once more*
> *see what a small coin it is*
> *against the darkness*
> —Mary Oliver

In Serifos, I was sure no sky could be so bright
as to swallow the sparrows' incessant chirrup
or bare the bronzed cliffs and cotton sheets
swollen with the ocean's humidity.
Each night I vanished into you only to find myself
in the morning. New body. New dangers.
The beaches were full of stones, would I be
only one of so many? At the monastery,
the silence might lift like the moon,
not with reassurance, but with familiarity,
like small birds buoyant in fright
who circle back to the nest, revealing their young.
Love hushed us into compliancy.
The monastery's marble floor cooled us
into shadows, modest votive offerings:
icons for the day, miracles for night.

viii

Figure of a Woman

It could have been the crescendo of summer:
the ebb and flow of your voice, the squid boats rocking
in the Bay of Livadi, sweet rakomelo on our lips.
Always when love comes hard, how it can fall.

The waves in the bay were like tongues
searching for an open mouth. What did I know
of your needs and you of mine. Now, you have
set the clock backwards and it is the ticking I listen for.
I don't want to become a deity. It holds
the word die. I lay that summer down
as a burnt offering.

                    Its smell is of hair, ocean,
and wild rosemary. I could let the whole island burn,
as if the dried gravel roads and beaches of nude bodies
had their own summer apart from us. You were cruel and wise.
I was nickels and beauty. I hear the sparrows still,
tidying their nests in the crooks of roofs. They were relentless.
The sky never clouded over, not once. I don't trust
a sky that won't rain. The rest of that year
crawled to me as if out of hiding.

III
Eternal City

When God demanded light,
he didn't banish darkness.
—Linda Pastan

I took you for the moon rising.
—W.S. Merwin

Listen

Like a hundred gray ears
the river stones are layered

in a pile near the shed where mourning
doves slow their peck and bobble to listen

to a chorus of listening.
Small buds on the lilac perk up.

A cardinal's torpedoed call comes
in slow waves of four,

round after round. It's a love call;
a call to make him known to himself.

The stones listen harder,
decipher the song; attempt

to offer back its echo.
But fail.

This is not a poem of coming spring.
This is a poem well aware

that gray flesh is dead flesh.
All of the ripe listening

comes at a cost. The first
sky is in all skies.

The first song
is in all songs.

San Bonaventura al Palatino, Rome

In the guitar player's notes shouldering
the path to San Bonaventura al Palatino
I hear scales of Franciscan Latin,
and as I walk past the gaping Roman ruins,
climb a slight winding slope, and once or twice
glance back into the wide-eyed stares
of the Roman Forum, I take pleasure
in knowing I will put down my cross
and never be nailed to this city nor any other.
The music seems to be clothed in vestments
of quiet plaster and ancient stone
as I enter the doorway of the friary.

The unblinking relief of the Stations of the Cross
carved within the wall marked
my journey and that of Christ's.
Can I rightly compare my suffering to his?
Embarking is harder than the return,
and the morning is often hardest:
the taste of empty hands
and a large vacant mouth,
a mouth large enough for the Eucharist
or a fist. Aqueducts of time and fortune
will water what I call my love. And I believe it.
All of it. *Hail Mary. Gratia plena.*
Dominus tecum. Gratia plena.
If I listen to Latin long enough,
I believe I speak it.

Ribollita

In a Tuscan farmhouse
I cook ribollita, a peasant soup
of white beans, crumbled bread, and kale,
as the campanile di San Biagio rings in the centuries.

Though not Catholic, maybe not even a Christian,
I kneel in the shadow of this church
and look deep inside the sleeves
of a sweater I've worn too many months.

After taking his own life,
the husband I knew burned
in a box I chose from several boxes.
I also chose his clothes, the urn,
and in the end asked for him
to look like death, not a false life.

Yet here I am, considering
a soup hundreds of years old,
the golden altar of the *Madonna de Buon Viaggio,*
and the sound of bells in the lower fields near our farm.
I know the path to the San Biagio
like I know the roof of my own mouth,
bells like foil between my teeth: electric.

The scent of footprints might confuse the dead,
but each night I end up between the sheets,
windows open in the last hour of lovemaking

among bed bugs and common centipedes.
In my new husband's arms,
trafficking old scars, I hear the prune plums
fall from the trees. I will collect
and skin them in the morning.

Golden Shovel Buddha

A warrior I am not, even when
I try my hardest. I am a disciple of we,
a follower of union, and I speak
clearly of the rickshaw of love to
anyone who'll listen. Each
of us must come to the edge of the other
either in this life or the next. Ours
is a marriage sifted from mistakes and old voices
ticked like a wristwatch: a reminder we are
on a well-worn path, king-sized and cherry like a
carved Buddha reclining in a gift shop window whose little
hands are like all hands, full of patience and a little gruff.

After *Untitled, 1969* by Mark Rothko

I travel to leave my pain in the city in which it belongs. Maybe the city of my birth or the city of my death. I travel to hear the melody of an instrument that no longer exists, or to see a boat launched by wives with candles, sons with less village. I travel to hell looking for an ashtray or thick black socks, a wristwatch I hope to wear and look at in order to keep up with time, but no matter how often I kiss eternity, it forsakes me. I am a daughter of two blind boats; I thought I was the daughter of two demi-gods. Rothko invites me

to weep at the foot of his painting, and I do. Using rabbit skin glue to prepare his canvases, he ensured the absence of distortion. But in raking light I am distortion. I am ashamed of my sorrow. No, I am ashamed of my memory. I travel to become two terrific rectangles, hovering over the coast of Maine, uneven margins, a rough edge, a palette of Arctic terns and herring gulls. Small brown rabbits venture to the lawn and sit like stones facing the shore. I travel, flanked and tall as a church, praying to the harmless and gravelly roads.

Ordo Virtutum

after Hildegard of Bingen

We fill our eyes when they are closed. We dig our fingers into the crevices of the flamed grain of the oak table in search of crumbs and pebbles of sand nested there. We hear the songs that come from these nests, clear and crisp as *Ordo Virtutum,* a music for the open mouths of Medieval women.

1st Class

We still struggle with our woman-soul. We will fill our empty arms. We will fill our empty bellies and our empty mouths. *Ordo Virtutum* will fill our empty ears. Our ears are always empty. We will never listen. We do not listen. We are women; we do not listen.

2nd Class

We empty our eyes when they are open. We will watch a ring and a ring weighed and bound. We will take and give these rings. We want the flint and fossil of the voice, but we know the voice is clear and crisp. The voice echoes like a rocking cathedral. The voice echoes like Amiens and Chartres.

3rd Class

We want a house as large as a cathedral. We want a house as dark and cold as a cathedral. We want a house as empty as a cathedral. We will fill our mouths when they are empty.

Supreme Class

We will fill our mouths with him and him and him. We will fill our mouths with the Father and the Son. We will taste the sharpness of the slaughter.

The Bride

She is not mouth and finger;
not footfalls and keys,
nor smolder, nor fortress of tulle and feather,
not tongue, not an amnesiac, nor a ringed exit;

she is not a laughing kitchen of oil and milk,
nor a funeral,
nor bracelets and hairpins;
she is not the quiver or the pitch.

She is not the stature of devils,
not the breastplate of afternoons,
not dread and insomnia,
not hen or egg.

The bride could never be the tureen
or the charger plate;
she is not corbels and prayers,
nor the sheet music
nor the watering on the wrist,

she is not the blade;
she is not the essay on Mayakovsky;
she is not the suggestion of Hopper in Truro;

she will not be harlequin,
nor the rose period,
nor will she be lashes and darling.

Absolution

In blue light, the newly married take everything
off, pleats and plaid fall to the floor,
windows open to the cold of night,
his hands warm as Sunday,
aching from the miles of minutes
between them, a communion
of the body, grace they need
from each other.

These winter nights are muted hopes,
like banked coals in the fireplace,
with McCoy Tyner on the stereo.

Who needs the ruthless words of seduction
or the molded clay of false affirmations?
Aren't they only rumor and ego anyway?
The metal front door lost
its handle years ago, but they
still lock and unlock
as they need to, and the clock
on the mantel directs the moon
through the room faster than ever.
Isn't it in the parlor of her body
he wants to abide?
Sleep will fall like snow.

Iconoclasm

*I approached the task of destroying images
by first tearing them out of the heart.*
—Martin Luther

We share a like-mindedness that grows tall and bends at the ceiling.
Like a mantra. Like liturgy. Like the global hum of hunger.

Taking whatever comes and taking it again and again:
the godliness of winter, the sinfulness of summer. We lay it all down.

We gloss over the fable where the girl falls into an endless sleep
because we both know death rested here, rested and waited awhile,

looking for other scraps, earthly and of flesh, but eventually moved on.
In the night, I spoke of his suicide: the shame of it,

his jaundiced eyes. The betrayal. The husband
no longer husband. Me belted to a narrative I didn't want.

The lash of the memory of love, the drenching
of new love, of flesh and bone, of kiss and kick.

I'll bake and knit and keep a house more precious than any house—
that I may place a prayer book open on my lap

as I recline by the cold fireplace like Mary in Campin's *Mérode Altarpiece*.
No one will provide a bench and a brass kettle, but you might equip me

with the myth of prurient lovers who over time find the smallest
detail of the other's body irresistible. My freckle, my thigh's curve.

I've been watching the grackles and now it's almost dark.
A light source allies us with the Dutch Masters.

We gaze easily over the fire at each other. In the small rooms
of our hearts, we both hide the false-gods of our past lives.

Forgetting the Masters

As the wind muscles up
to my nude body at Playalinda Beach,
I wonder what it is like to be a man,
ball sack sunburned and salt rimmed,
everything I think I need outside of myself.

I wear only my new husband's name, even as
the ocean's baritone waves pry the shell of me
open and fill me from head to toe
with the collapsing syllables of the Patriarch.
I forget God, rowboats, masters of silent art.

When I cut lemon for our tea, I slice my finger
and it stings from the juice. It is my husband,
as he cups my breast, who tells me
that the smallest cuts heal with no scar. I believe him.
I believe every word: a blanket for my memory,
especially when it turns cold. Like a water stain,
the tide inches closer. The pelicans lift and align
like the typed letters of my new name.

Duccio's *Annunciation*

What else might Gabriel have said
to Mary after he recoiled his right hand
and folded his two coffee-colored wings
into themselves? Did he admire the thin
leggy lilies between them, or point out
the Holy Spirit, well on his way,
diving under the cusped arch?

I love the idea of the messenger:
someone who will make the drive,
mail the letter, tell it like it is.
In the daylight, gray is always
reconciled by blue. Even if the window
is weak and leaks too much road noise:
gray will give way with a little coaxing.

Yesterday, hail fell hard
like chattering teeth. When I'm cold
or nervous, I am a sky that shudders
and shakes, a sky that can't sit still.

Although it is autumn,
today we are at the beach,
have shed all our clothes.
It is enough to be naked,
and lie on the blanket
like warmed coins,
our eyes like old suns.
The surf is rough from the storm

as the waves, like giants,
jostle for a kingdom.
In Italy we learned
there were no beaches
on which we could bare all.
Instead, we found a church
and said a few prayers.

That night I washed the fall pears.
I couldn't wait to sink my teeth
into their gritty flesh.

Surprise Concert at Musée des Beaux Arts, Montreal

It's a harpsichord, not a piano.
Most pianos aren't painted like the fresco
of Livia's Roman garden, nor are they
this extraordinarily long. My husband
has surprised me with a concert and the stars
this afternoon are the harpsichord and cello:
Sonata No. 2 in C Minor walks onto the stage
like an old man in velvet with a white beard,
notes from the eighteenth-century peak
like the Viennese ranges the composer
Franciscello eventually called home.

Montreal is leading the dance in the north,
and I am happy to follow—
waltzing backwards isn't as hard as I thought.
I awake the next day to white and white
outside our twenty-second-floor hotel-room window,
snow flying like large insects with somewhere to be,
like mayflies with twenty-four hours to eat,
mate, and die. The ring on my finger
reminds me that this is what we will do tonight,
and tomorrow night, and the next. Happily.
It is warm here in our Canadian blizzard.
I'll catch a cab with one gloved hand,
the other pocketed and ready for a new season,
the cello and harpsichord dancing
together a verdict of yes. Whenever I can, I keep time,
but the numbers mean nothing, as they should.
Neither of us can carry the snow or its white weight.

The Canadian Robins on Epiphany

I didn't know robins remained
in Vermont through the winter,
but here at early dusk
they animate like skipping stones,
lift and drop from one pine to the next,
cave into the cedars:
winged miners after something gold.

My cousin needs me to talk.
Her friend's nineteen-year-old son
killed himself just twelve days after Christmas.
I tell her there is no way to turn
the burner down. For the living: the stove is on high,
the burns will come and seem unbearable,
but the skin will slough off, waxen,
scar. If we are lucky,
we will crawl out of our dark bodies,
apply a balm to our wounds. As she talks,
I wonder how a moth has frozen to the window, white
translucent. I might have missed it for the snow.

North of the Past

Small pellets of ice
confetti my windowpane
as the cedars slough off their snow
as if deciding against Winter's
communion, as if releasing
one universal sigh,
tired of rising always
as nature's architecture.
With wisdom, I am only pretending.
Who was weeping two nights ago?
Sometimes I don't recognize
my own sobs.

After the funeral, when I opened
my husband's urn,
I accidentally spilled some of the ash.
Not knowing what to do,
I licked my palm and fingers,
my own sacrament.

But that was years ago.
Now, week after week I skip
out on church, despite the crows
calling from the treetops.
The North forgives
my absence. Maybe it's all
the white or maybe
it's just the knuckle
bone of the wind.

The Love Movement

i

Water Rings

Laughter, like the pages of a paperback, tears easily.
For you, I'd meet my maker in the darkened corner
of a bar. Love, can I ask you? Your answers are
what tables are made of, your answers leave water
rings, my questions knock us into the reupholstered
day, tacked and stapled by the sun, seat-worn to
a gracious grin. You are as strong as a bronzed
necklace of bones; your hands have lived inside a
famine of caresses. How true for us: modern sails are
rarely made of natural fibers; age-old cloth is porous
enough for a soul to pass. Howling into the path,
your voice bears bunkers. You, survivor of pitch and
war, of fire and fear, pick the pilgrimage. And, can I
ask you? You are the jailer of tea and time, right? So
where will I reside in this era of letters, where will I
reside in this era of love?

Tournesol

She comes to the edge of the road near the *Abbaye de Valmagne,* the one lined with sunflowers and a type of tree that reminds her of the springing and transverse arches of cathedral interiors, reminds her of where pleasure and the color blue are simultaneous in the body, where stained glass and flight might be confused. She jars her thoughts and labels them for later when she'll share a cigarette and a glass from the region. Who wouldn't adore Southern France? The arid postures of the hilltop abbeys and the crisp courtyards of the new *vin rosé*? Dusk doesn't douse the day until 9:00, leaving enough time for the sunflowers to unwind, end the paralysis of the summer's dead weight. She looks left, then right, deciding between two hemispheres in a province where roads are named for philosophers and poets.

With Major on Hawk Mountain

In the early evening the sky blushes
at our close attention. We can't
take our eyes off of it
as two mourning doves lift and land
near our empty feeder,
paired for life. The male lilts
a coo, his breast mirrors the pink above us.
I begin to hum a song,
something about icons and suitcases.
Last summer I collected the dead
monarch that now rests like a Medieval relic
on the yellow paper on my desk. One wing is split
in two, a female with thick kohl veins
and no black dot on the hindwings:
like Tiffany glass all fire and pitch.
The milkweed she ate all summer
turned her blood to poison
for her predators. Now, her wings are as brittle
as book pages left in the rain, dried in the sun.
The summer my previous husband took
his life I thought each monarch in our garden was a sign.
Not so. Dead is dead.
The flush mountains now look as if
they want a short nap, might come to life
later with the moonlight. Even the dove
has quieted into his shared nest.

Moon Jar

My wedding ring is missing
one small diamond, and

I like it that way: a reminder
of the imperfect in

all of us, like that keyhole
size of grief that remains crystalline.

In Korea, ceramicists for centuries
have made moon jars, testimony

to the virtue of modesty: asymmetrical
warping on the wheel, slumping

in the pine-heated kiln,
impurities when fired—black

dots and pocks on its surface
like freckles on skin.

I have been kept awake
so many nights by the moon:

its pull on the pines and night birds
and who, like a monk, keeps a sharp order of time.

Never a perfect sphere,
the milky moon jar joins two

clay hemispheres into one.
When the light of the moon

finds me, I am the color
of everything in the winter night.

ACKNOWLEDGMENTS

I am grateful to the editors of the following publications in which versions of these poems first appeared:

The *Café Review*: "Your Husband Was a City in a Country of Sorrow"; *The Common* (print): "Killing Jar"; *The Common* (online): "San Bonaventura" and "Almost Animal"; *Green Mountains Review* (online): "Absolution" and "Warning Signs"; *Green Mountains Review* (print): "Encaustic" and "The Hole in the Earth"; *Iowa Review*: "Honing" and "After the Suicide"; *New South*: "Epistle to My Late Husband after an Evening with My Fiancé"; the *New Yorker*: "Signs for the Living"; *Ploughshares*: "The Sandhill Crane"; *Solstice*: "*Ordo Virtutum*," "The Bride," and "*kill lies all*"; *Southern Indiana Review*: "Moon Jar"; and *Water~ Stone Review*: "The Almond Bush."

"Listen" was featured on the podcast *The Slow Down* with Tracy K. Smith, produced by America Pubic Media with funding from the Poetry Foundation and support from the Library of Congress.

"Golden Shovel Buddha" was anthologized in *Golden Shovel Anthology: New Poems Honoring Gwendolyn Brooks*, University of Arkansas Press, 2017.

"Ribollita" was anthologized in *World English Poetry Anthology*, Bengal Publications LTD, 2016.

"Lot's Wife," "Iconoclasm," and "The Love Movement" first appeared as part of the chapbook *Slag and Fortune*, Floating Wolf Press, 2013.

I would foremost like to thank the many poets who were brave enough to write about suicide and their grief. Your work is an inspiration to me, and I thank you for giving me permission to tell my own story. I hope this book might help others who have found themselves facing the darkness of being a suicide survivor.

Also, thank you to those teachers and mentors whose feedback on my poems has been invaluable. From Bennington Writing Seminars: Tracy K. Smith, Mark Wunderlich, David Daniel, Nathalie Handal, and April Bernard. A special thank you to Sidney Wade who, in yellow knee-highs and Dansko clogs, first inspired me to write poetry; to Don Stap who was always in my corner and supporting my work; and to Bruce Aufhammer whose words of encouragement helped me to believe I was an actual poet.

A special deep gratitude for the encouragement and long friendship of Michele Randall who, for over twenty years, met with me on Monday nights at my dining room table to write poems. I am indebted to Tanya Grae for her friendship and keen eye even at our weekly 7:00 a.m. Sunday poetry breakfasts. To my Coven: Carolyn, Patricia, Susan, Suzanne, Sholeh, and Ilyse. To each brilliant member of the poetry group in Vermont, especially to Liz Powell and Kerrin McCadden for being *good babies* always.

Thank you, Kate Gale, for believing in this book. And thank you to everyone at Red Hen Press who helped with my vision. And thank you to Jane Kent for the stunning artwork for the cover.

I am blessed and grateful to come from a community who, in one way or another, supported me over the years with my writing and helped me survive. Thank you (in alphabetical order) to Morgen Aiken, Marnie Burkett, Chris Croft-Crossland, Michele Dershimer, Danielle Gasparro, Jeff Huckaby, Stacy Mellick, Victoria Meyers, and Terry Thaxton.

A special thank you to my mother, Lois Gibbs-Joyce, for her support and for always being there by my side to mourn loss and to celebrate new beginnings. And to all my family, thank you for your eternal support: Bob Joyce, Nikki Schonert who is like my sister, Shelia and Al Schonert, Thelma McCarthy, Jennifer Joyce, and Amy Krazeise. We might be a small family, but we are strong. I also want to say how grateful I am now to share my life with Langston McCullough, Anastasia White, and Romie Jackson. You bring me such happiness. Thank you all for your love and support.

My immense pride and appreciation to my son, Dylan. Your strength and love are what helped me to persevere when I wasn't sure I could go on. I hope I was strong for you too. You are my greatest joy. Thank you also to Lian Jacobs. I am so grateful for your presence.

Finally, I want to thank my husband, Major Jackson. It is your unending belief in me and my writing that keeps me going. You are my biggest fan, and I am yours. What a blessed life we share. Thank you for always being my first reader and my first critic. And thank you for your immense love. I feel it every day.

Biographical Note

Didi Jackson's poems have appeared in the *New Yorker, New England Review, Ploughshares,* and elsewhere. After having lived most of her life in Florida, she currently lives in South Burlington, Vermont, and teaches creative writing at the University of Vermont.